PEGGY

MERRY CHRISTMAS, 2006

LOVE,
DEAN

COW DOGS

THE COWBOY'S BEST FRIEND

Birthday Party
Zollinger Ranch, Idaho

COW DOGS

THE COWBOY'S BEST FRIEND

Photography by David R. Stoecklein

STOECKLEIN PUBLISHING

COW DOGS

THE COWBOY'S BEST FRIEND

PHOTOGRAPHY	DAVID R. STOECKLEIN
TEXT	SHIRL WOODSON
EDITOR	CARRIE JAMES
ART DIRECTION & DESIGN	T-GRAPHICS

Cover Photo - Yokohl Ranch, California
Back Cover Photo - Jess Valley Ranch, California

All images in this book are available as signed original gallery prints and for stock photography usage. Stoecklein Photography houses an extensive stock library of Western, sports, and lifestyle images. Dave Stoecklein is also an assignment photographer whose clients include Canon, Kodak, Bayer, Hatteras, Marlboro, Chevrolet, Timberland, Ford, Wrangler, Pontiac, and the Cayman Islands.

Other books by Stoecklein Publishing include The Idaho Cowboy, Cowboy Gear, Don't Fence Me In, The Texas Cowboys, The Montana Cowboy, The Western Horse, Cowgirls, Spirit of the West, The California Cowboy, The Performance Horse, Lil' Buckaroos, and The American Paint Horse.

Every year, Stoecklein Publishing also produces a line of wall calendars, prints, and cards featuring the Western photography of David R. Stoecklein. For more information or to request a catalog, please contact

Stoecklein Publishing & Photography
Tenth Street Center, Suite A1
Post Office Box 856 • Ketchum, Idaho 83340
tel 208.726.5191 fax 208.726.9752 toll free 800.727.5191
www.stoeckleinphotography.com

published by World Publishing Services
2135 Wilder Street • Helena, Montana 59601

Printed in China

Copyright ©2002 by David R. Stoecklein & Stoecklein Publishing

ISBN 1-931153-20-5
Library of Congress Catalog number 2002091148

previous page
Hubing Ranch, Montana

Wade Plainer
White Bird, Idaho

Introduction

On a cold day in January of 1992, I found myself standing on top of a mountain pass in Grangeville, Idaho. With me were my two assistants, Jim and Bruce, as well as our host, the legendary saddle builder, Ray Holes, and my sidekick cowboy, Monte Funkhouser. It had snowed the night before and the clouds were lifting just enough for us to see the distant ridge. We were waiting for Wade Plainer, a cowboy who was spending the winter down on the Snake River. He was bringing a herd of cattle that he had rounded up and was on his way back to the ranch.

Around noon, Wade radioed us to say that he was about to come over the crest of the mountain. At that point, we saw him and his dogs bringing the cattle through the snow. Wade asked me where I wanted to photograph the herd and I pointed over to the other side of the hill. I was worried that it might be close to impossible for him to move all of the cattle and get them in the right position. Not only did Wade move them to the right place, but he was able to move them again and again, wherever I asked. This was the first time I ever got to see real cow dogs work. These were trained dogs and they could do whatever Wade asked them to do.

Since that day, I have seen all kinds of cow dogs at work and at play. I have watched how they interact with their masters, play with the ranch kids, chase the barn cats, and frighten the chickens. Cow dogs have the most distinctive personalities and are the most intelligent, most loyal, and funniest dang dogs in the world. They come in all different sizes, shapes, colors, and breeds.

This book was a real kick to put together. The collection of photos has been growing ever since that day I spent with Wade and his dogs on that Idaho mountaintop so long ago. A few years ago, I published my first Cow Dogs calendar that has now become an annual tradition. I always knew that some day I would expand that project and do a book on cow dogs as well. I hope these photographs bring you joy and laughter and that they stir up some memories of all the loyal, hard-working canine companions that have crossed your path.

This book is a heartfelt tribute to the working cow dog.

What is a Cow Dog?

Text by Shirl Woodson

The partnership between man and dog began early in the pages of recorded time. Physical evidence shows that the canine roamed the countryside of Iraq as early as 14,000 years ago. Commonly thought to be the descendent of the wolf, the dog was a common sight near the camps of primitive men. Dogs soon learned that these locations provided a good spot to scavenge for food. Men were also quick to learn the advantage of having dogs in close proximity. Packs of dogs made efficient hunting teams. When men and dogs joined forces, they both often enjoyed the spoils of the kill. As time went on, men discovered that dogs, like people, possess individual talents. It wasn't long before the most desirable dog was one that not only had an instinct for alerting the camp of the arrival of intruders, but also had the natural ability to gather and herd stock. This dog came to be known as the shepherd's dog.

The shepherd and his flock is a common subject in both the Old and New Testaments. However, the shepherd's dog is rarely mentioned in Biblical text. The birthplace of Judaism, Christianity, and Islam was also the site of the domestication of the dog. In the beginning, all three religions were in agreement regarding the treatment of dogs. A dog was not considered a treasured companion, but a filthy nuisance. A dog was merely a beast that devoured garbage and human corpses and carried dangerous germs. To be called the "son of a dog" was at the top of the list of vile epitaphs issued by one man to another. The only dog to receive favorable comment in Biblical text is the shepherd's dog. Mirroring the sentiment reflected in the Bible, Mohammed, the Great Prophet of Islam, decreed that all dogs were "unclean" and should be killed. The only exceptions were the shepherd's dog and the hunting dog.

Dogs of Biblical times bear scant resemblance to the modern day stock dog. Early dogs were shorthaired and aggressive. Their duties included guarding as well as herding stock. The shepherd's dog alerted its master to any nighttime intruders. The dog's ability to keep animals grouped together allowed the shepherd the freedom to pursue a nomad's life.

By 100 B.C., the herding dog was an important part of the stockman's life. In the book *De Re Rustic* from 116 B.C., Marcus Terentius Varro describes the value of this dog. Varro discusses in detail how to purchase a herding dog as well as how many dogs a herder requires in various situations. Roman herding dogs are thought to be descendants of dogs from the countries of Asia or Tibet. The Roman dogs were large black and tan brutes that were a cross between Molossian-type dogs from these countries and the smaller Bedouin sheepdogs of Biblical times. Their primary duty was to guard the herds and flocks of the stockmen.

When the Romans invaded Britain in A.D. 43, they brought both their livestock and their herding dogs. As that empire declined, the Vikings and the Anglos and the Saxons of Germany took the place of the ousted Romans. They too brought their dogs. The Border Collie, the Fox Collie, and the Sheltie are just some of the breeds from the British Isles that are similar to the Norwegian Toonie and the Lapponian Herder. It is likely that these dogs were transported to and from Britain during the war years, altering the various strains of herd dogs. The British working collies of the 1700s and 1800s came from the mixing of Roman and Viking dogs with Polish lowland dogs. The term "collie" from that day refers to a general working farm dog, not an individual breed of dog such as the Border Collie or the Bearded Collie.

A distinction was made between the herder's dog and the shepherd's dog in 1486 in the *Book of St. Albans*. In this work, the shepherd's dog was called "tryndel tayles" or long-tailed. The drover's dog was the cur dog with a bobbed tail. Usually a cross between a collie and a foxhound or mastiff, the drover's dog was a heavier dog used to move cattle and wilder breeds of sheep. Drover's dogs were tax-exempt as herding dogs. They bore docked tails to prove their tax-exempt status. They became known as curs, meaning curtailed or dock-tailed. The system was abandoned in 1796 when it became evident that dogs other than the drover's dogs were being docked so that their owners could avoid taxation.

Different types of terrain, different types of stock, and different sizes of pastures all became essential factors in a herder's choice of dog. As a result of selective breeding to suit the needs of an individual herder or shepherd, various breeds of stock dogs emerged. The most popular of these dogs currently used in the United States by ranchers are the Australian Kelpie, the Australian Cattle Dog, the Australian Shepherd, the Border Collie, the McNab, and the Catahoula Leopard Dog.

The Australian Kelpie was first introduced in Australia in the mid-1800s. Breeders mixed different strains of working collies with Australia's native dingo. The end result was a dog that could gather and hold stock as well as help the owner

8

Wade Plainer
White Bird, Idaho

9

Hollister Ranch, California

move herds from place to place. The Australian Kelpie was also perfectly suited to the harsh Australian terrain and the blistering heat. Since most general working farm dogs were still referred to as collies, even kelpie pups purchased from noted breeders were called Kelpie Collies in their early years in Australia.

The exact mix of breeds in this energetic dog have become the subject of dispute. What is known is that a bitch owned by a man named Jack Gleeson was named Kelpie. Gleeson, recognized for his love of fine horses and good dogs, admired a strain of dogs used on George Robertson's Worrock Station in Western Victoria. He especially liked a black and tan female pup and attempted to purchase the dog. The owner refused his request until Gleeson offered to trade one of his fine stock horses for the young pup. Her pedigree was unknown, but it was reputed that she might have had a trace of dingo blood. Her long black hair had a reddish tinge, her ears were lopped and she was of medium size. When she worked, her ears went up and down. Gleeson named the pup Kelpie. In Gaelic, the word "kelpie" means a malevolent water sprite in the form of a horse. Robert Louis Stevenson included the archaic word in his popular book of the 1800s, *Kidnapped*. In the book, Stevenson writes: "The Water Kelpie, the demon of the streams who is fabled to keep wailing and roaring at the ford until the coming of the doomed traveller (sic)." Like the kelpie of lore, the dog is as quick and agile as a water sprite and as spirited as a horse. When it stares at a man or beast, its intense look can produce shivers.

After trading for Kelpie, Gleeson made his way to North Bolero to take a position as an overseer. Along the way, he met his friend Mark Tully who was the manager of a station on Billabong Creek. Tully was a good dog man and a great fan of the Rutherford strain of collies. Tully gave Gleeson a dog by the name of Moss. Moss was a smooth-haired, black dog with pricked ears. The sire and dam of Moss were imported from Scotland and came from Rutherford Collies. Not connected with the formation of the Border Collie breed, the Rutherford strain can trace its history back hundreds of years to the highlands of Scotland. When Rutherford family members migrated to Australia, they brought their collies with them. Many refer to Rutherford Collies as Fox Collies because of their fox-like faces and occasional red coloring.

In the 1870s, William Allen of Geralda Station in New South Wales imported two dogs called Brutus and Jennie, also from Scotland. Brutus was a big dog with a smooth coat. He was black and tan in color with pricked ears. Jennie was long-haired and had half-erect ears. Their puppies were all black and tan with the exception of one red pup. All modern day chestnut or red kelpies are thought to be that one pup's descendants. Brutus and Jennie soon made a name for themselves as quiet workers who could contain the nervous, hard-running Australian merino sheep. They ran wide around the flock and used a lot of eye contact to control them.

One of Brutus and Jennie's first pups, Caesar, was mated to Gleeson's Kelpie. The most famous offspring of that breeding was the black and tan bitch known as King's Kelpie. King's Kelpie gained fame for winning first place in the 1879 sheepdog trial held at the Forbes Show. King's Kelpie was also the granddame of Barb, a dog named after the black horse that won the Melbourne Cup in 1869.

The demand for pups from Gleeson's dogs grew quickly and soon he was besieged with requests for kelpie pups. It is the opinion of many that the best kelpies can be traced back to Gleeson's Kelpie, King's Kelpie, and Moss. It is not known when or how much dingo was added to the early bloodlines. Modern Australian Kelpies are tireless herding and head dogs. They are extremely intelligent and athletic. Kelpies are known for rapid starts, dead stops, and an ability to travel long distances away from a master and still take direction. So strong is a kelpie's natural inclination to work that they would probably rather work than eat. They handle not only sheep, but also cattle, horses, or anything else that moves. Although they are primarily head dogs, they will heel as well. The dogs are true workaholics. They take the greatest pleasure in work for work's sake and their reward is not in pleasing owners, but in pleasing themselves by working.

Kelpies have short, straight coats with weather-resistant outer coats. They range in colors including black, black and tan, red, red and tan, dark chestnut, blue-gray, fawn, or cream. Often kelpies' eyes are blue or yellowish. They have fox-like faces and upright ears and their yellow-tinted eyes sometimes make them appear almost demonic, often an unnerving feature to those unfamiliar with the breed.

The harsh climate and terrain of the Australian Outback led to the development of another popular stock dog, the Australian Cattle Dog. In the States, this dog is often referred to as the Australian Heeler, Queensland Heeler, or Blue Heeler. The development of the Australian Cattle Dog most likely began when a man by the name of Timmons crossed a Smithfield Collie with a dingo. The dogs resulting from this cross were called Timmons Biters. The red, bobtailed dogs were admired for their ability to work silently; however, they had a nasty habit of delivering severe bites. If an owner were out of sight, the temptation for the dog to kill calves would be too great, often resulting in misfortune for calf and owner. The next attempt to make a suitable Australian Cattle Dog came about when the dingo was mixed with a Rough Collie. This was not a good match either. The dogs barked at the head of the cattle, stirring the stock into a frenzy. Cattle going to market often became agitated and lost weight.

In 1840, Thomas Hall of Muswelbrook, New South Wales imported Blue Smooth Highland Collies to Australia. These dogs were blue merles, very similar to the modern Bearded Collie. The merle is an ancient color dating to the Saxon invasion of Britain. It became such a common color that for a time, working merle collies were destroyed for being too common. The pups from the dogs he imported were bred with the dingo. The resulting puppies were blue or red-speckled. This cross was known as a Hall's Heeler. This stocky dog would silently creep up on an animal, then bite and flatten itself against the ground to avoid being kicked. Also during this decade, a man named Tom Bentley acquired a dog from Mr. Hall. The dog was known as Bentley's Dog for its outstanding working ability. Used as a stud dog as well as a working dog, Bentley's Dog is given credit for the white blaze on the forehead of many modern Australian Cattle Dogs. The blaze is still referred to as a Bentley Mark. Bentley's Dog also contributed the black tail root spot commonly seen on blue dogs of this breed.

In the 1870s, a butcher by the name of Fred Davis bought a pair of Hall's Heelers to work in Sydney stockyards. For a time, Davis tried putting a little Bull Terrier blood into the mix. That was phased out when Davis discovered that once the dogs bit, they did not let go. Then Jack and Harry Bagust decided to add some Dalmatian blood to the breed. Their reasoning behind this was that Dalmatians love horses and are very loyal. The brothers were also thought to have added some kelpie blood. Today the influence of both the Bull Terrier and the Dalmatian is still evident. Australian Cattle Dog puppies are born white like Dalmatians and when they reach maturity, they often have broad heads like Bull Terriers. The Australian Cattle Dog has evolved into a breed of dog known for its skill in heeling cattle. They possess a natural ability to fetch as well as a strong guarding instinct. This sturdy, compact dog is often either blue merle or red-speckled in color. It may also have black, blue, or tan markings on its head.

Similar to the Australian Cattle Dog is the Australian Stumpy Tail Cattle Dog, also called the Smithfield Heeler. Although often confused with the Australian Cattle Dog, the Stumpy Tail is a separate breed. These dogs have square bodies and more finely shaped heads than Australian Cattle Dogs. The Stumpy Tail cattle dog has smaller, high-set ears and a tail not longer than four inches when fully grown. A Stumpy Tail does not have any tan in its markings. Like the Australian Cattle Dog, the Stumpy Tail cattle dog has both dingo and Blue Merle Collie blood. However, there is no evidence of Bull Terrier or the black and tan sheepdog. Its heritage leads directly to the Timmons Biter, the early cross of the Smithfield Collies and the dingo. The Timmons Biter was later crossed with a smooth-haired Blue Merle Collie in an attempt to lesson the amount of bite in the breed.

Unlike the Australian Kelpie, the Australian Cattle Dog, and the Stumpy Tail cattle dog, the Australian Shepherd actually originated in the United Sates. The name comes from its association with the Basque shepherds who immigrated to the United States via Australia. The Basque herders initially left the cane plantations of Australia to come to California in a quest for gold. Many of these men eventually left the gold fields and returned to their homeland to herd sheep. With the arrival of the Gold Rush in California, and later the Civil War, the need for larger flocks of sheep developed. These events pushed the demand for wool and mutton in the United Sates to an all-time high. To meet these needs, sheep were brought to the West from the Midwest and New Mexico. The flocks were driven across wild, undeveloped land to California. Other flocks from the East Coast and Australia made their way west via sailing ships traveling around Cape Horn.

Along with the sheep came the dogs to herd them. The New Mexican Sheepdogs, as they were called, were large and powerful. Fierce guard dogs, they resembled wolves. Generally, they were a yellowish-white color. The dogs from the eastern part of the country were of the old-fashioned collie variety. Some of them came to this country directly from Britain. These dogs were usually black with white or tan markings.

The dogs coming with the flocks from Australia were also descendants of those who had arrived there from Britain. Most common were the Smithfield Collie and the German Coolie. The Smithfield Collie is a rough-coated dog with a bobbed tail. The Australian Shepherd of today usually has a tail docked to a length of about four inches. Early on, there were pockets of German Coolies in Australia. These dogs were most likely delivered to Australia from Saxony by German immigrants. The German Coolie is usually a merle.

Cross breeding eventually resulted in the Australian Shepherd breed. Various strains of herd dogs were crossbred in the American West during the late 1800s and early 1900s. The Australian Shepherd is predominately a descendant of the collie/shepherd dogs from the British Isles with a small amount of Spanish/Basque influence. The Australian Shepherd is a medium-sized dog and is blue merle, red merle, solid black, or solid red in color. Like the old collie colors of the English Shepherd, the Australian Shepherd of today is

King Ranch, Texas

often tri-colored—black and tan or black and white. They often have white or copper-colored trim. The eyes of the Australian Shepherd are usually blue, brown, or marbled. They are easy to train, gentle, eager to please, and very loyal family dogs.

The term "collie," as it applies to the herd dog, is the subject of much conjecture. In Gaelic, "collie" means something useful. Some think the word was originally "coalie." In the 1911 book *The Shepherds of Britain*, Adelaide L.J. Gosset states that the word "collie" was derived from the black color of coal. Gosset's reasoning was that many of the herd dogs were black and the legs and the faces of the Scottish sheep were black. In Great Britain, "colley" or "coly" mean soot, smut, or coal dust—all symbols of the color black. Another theory is that the German word "kuli" is the source of the term. "Kuli" is pronounced the same as "coolie" which refers to a laborer. Still others believe that "kuli" is an Anglo-Saxon word for a useful dog. The herd dog is often as helpful to its master as another hired man is. Whether the word means useful, black-colored, or laborer, all readily apply to what has become one of the most popular stock dogs in the United States—the Border Collie.

Since its arrival in this country, the Border Collie has assumed an important role on farms and ranches across the country. Identified as the most intelligent breed of dog, this affectionate, loyal dog can be easily trained for a variety of tasks. Gentle by nature, the Border Collie is very people oriented and obedient. This dog loves to work, play, and please its owner. Praise and attention are two of the things the Border Collie thrives upon. The Border Collie quickly learns the routine of the day. Often, it anticipates its owner's next move even before receiving instruction and is quite capable of independent thinking.

Bred to gather and fetch, the Border Collie instinctively runs wide around the herd rather than disturbing the animals by getting too close. Although the head dog prefers to bring animals back to the herder, it can be taught to drive stock away from its master as well. Although it is further removed genetically from the wolf than a primitive man's dog, the Border Collie sometimes displays wolf-like traits when working. Like the wolf, the Border Collie instinctively crouches down with its haunches higher than the front of its body. With its head lowered and staring intently, the dog can take command of a sheep or cow through controlled intimidation. By fiercely eyeing its target, it can assert its dominance even before moving the animal. A strong eye can have a hypnotic effect on a dog's target. For sheep and cows, a dog's eye is purely a predatory warning sign. A Border Collie will often circle wide like a wolf in the wild and then crouch down, belly to the ground directly in front of the animal they intend to stop or turn. Crouching down and a strong eye are strong deterrents to a prospective escapee.

The Border Collie is one of the newest strains of collie and its roots run deep. Dr. John Caius wrote the *De Canibus Britannicus* (Treatise on Englishe Dogges) in 1570. In his writings, he clearly describes an ancestor of the modern day Border Collie. Known then as "the shepherd's dog," historians agree that Caius was writing about a genetic predecessor to the Border Collie. *De Canibus Britannicus* is recognized as one of the earliest books to describe in detail the characteristics of British sheepdogs.

Artwork of the 1700s and 1800s often depicts herding dogs that bear a strong resemblance to the modern Border Collie. Literature of that time also reflected similarities to the modern Border Collie. Thomas Bewick published *The General History of The Quadruped* in 1790. In the book, Bewick describes the shepherd's dog as a rough-coated dog, black in color, with a white ring around its neck and a white tip on its tail. Bewick also writes that drover's dogs and shepherd's dogs were called "coally dogs."

The modern Border Collie is most commonly black and white in color with a ring around its neck. It may also be tri-colored: black, white, and tan. There are also red and white or blue and white Border Collies in addition to blue or red merles. Today the dogs generally weigh between 35 and 50 pounds. Usually their eyes are dark in color, and occasionally a Border Collie will have one blue eye and one dark eye.

James Reid, secretary of the International Sheepdog Society from 1915 to 1948, coined the name Border Collie in 1918. The best working collie lines of that time were found in the great border sheep runs. In 1946, following World War II, Reid put the word "Border" on registration papers of working collies registered by the International Sheepdog Society. This addition stemmed from the need to distinguish this working dog from its show ring counterpart. Until the mid 1800s, there was much cross breeding of herding dogs in Great Britain and Europe. Before the existence of breed registries for the Border Collie, this type of dog was known as a working or unimproved collie.

Throughout the history of the stock dog, we have seen many different types of collies. There are Smooth-Coated Collies, Rough-Coated Collies, Fox Collies, Bearded Collies, Old English Sheepdogs, Harlequin Collies, Shetland Sheepdogs, and Pembroke and Cardigan Welsh Corgis. Dogs herding livestock in the British Isles have been called Working

Yokohl Ranch, California

Collies, Old-Fashioned Collies, Farm Collies, and English Collies. Some of the collie breeds of the past are no longer in existence. Changes in the needs of the shepherds and the drovers brought about changes in what types of dogs were needed to work stock. For instance, the unique demands of the shepherds in the border counties of England and Scotland brought about the development of the Border Collie breed. These dogs are the product of line breeding and inbreeding. Large dogs were needed in the lowland areas where great flocks of heavier sheep grazed. Rough mountain terrain dotted with wild, nervous sheep required a smaller, more agile dog.

Another type of collie that developed into a breed of its own is the McNab. The McNab is descended from the working collies in the Grampian Hills of central Scotland. When Alexander McNab came to Mendocino, California from that area in 1868, he brought one of the native dogs with him from his homeland. Unfortunately, this dog died shortly after his arrival. McNab journeyed back to the Grampian Hills in 1885. Before he returned to California, he purchased two Scotch Collies or Fox Shepherds, Peter and Fred. Peter (who was both a lead and drive dog) sailed to the States with Alex. Fred (a lead dog only) stayed on in Scotland to have his training completed and made the journey later.

Once the dogs were settled in, Alex bred them to shepherd females of Spanish origin. Quickly, the dogs of the McNab family became extremely popular. In 1895, Ed Brown ordered a McNab pup. His order was not filled until 1915 due to the high demand. Brown's pup Jet was black with a faint line of white up the middle of its face and white markings on its chest and feet. The McNab family soon chose to import shorthaired dogs that were better suited to the warm California climate. Not only was the area hot in the summer, but the terrain also had lots of foxtails, burs, and other stickers to tangle the coat of a longhaired dog. McNabs are generally black with white collars, chests, and legs. A tip of white often marks its tail. The heritage of Ed Brown's dog Jet is often evident in the white stripe down the center of a pup's black face. These dogs are cat-footed, energetic, and extremely intelligent. It is never clear if a master chooses the dog or if the dog chooses its master. In either case, the McNab is usually a one-man dog.

Not all herd dogs can be traced to the British Isles. A descendant of one of the first domestic dogs brought to the New World is the Catahoula Leopard dog. Over four hundred years ago, Spain made explorations of the Gulf Coast and the southern portion of the East Coast of the United States. The Spaniards brought dogs of war with them. These dogs were most likely of Mastiff and Greyhound blood. The dogs of war were used for hunting, guarding the soldiers' camps, and on the battlefield. When the soldiers left this region, they left behind some of their dogs. The red wolf that was native to the area then bred with the abandoned war dogs, producing offspring that became the companions of Native Americans. When the French arrived one hundred years later, they discovered wolf-like dogs with haunting, light-colored eyes. These dogs were bred with the Beauceron dog, which had accompanied the Frenchmen to the New World. The Beauceron dates back to the 1500s and was highly regarded for its ability to hunt wild boar. The resulting cross of the Spanish war dogs, the red wolf, and the Beauceron is now known as the Catahoula Leopard dog, a single-coated, shorthaired, merle or black and tan-patterned dog.

The Catahoula Leopard dog has a keen sense of smell. Its webbed feet make it a natural at gathering wild cattle in marshy areas. This breed has a natural ability to herd and gather livestock. The ideal way to work this breed of herd dog is in groups of three. Together they find cattle and hold them still, while baying to signify success. If a cow breaks out of the herd, they will circle around her until she rejoins the rest of the group. They are head dogs.

Many of the dogs found on the ranches of the American West can trace their lineage to one of the breeds heretofore mentioned. Usually a rancher, like a shepherd of old, has determined what breeds produce the best cross to suit his needs. If the cross does not work out, he tries a slightly different mix. No matter whether a dog is purebred or a homespun cross, the rancher and the herd dog are inseparable. They are a team. No American ranch is complete without the presence of a stock dog.

Yokohl Ranch, California

YO Ranch, Texas

18

Pate Ranch, Montana

"I hope she doesn't expect me to get in there."

Mesa Pate
Pate Ranch, Montana

Ellison Ranches, Nevada

22

Zollinger Ranch, Idaho

"I'm hot
and
thirsty."

Hollister Ranch, California

Yokohl Ranch, California

previous page
Jay Hoggan, Dan Lock
Hoggan Ranch, Hamer, Idaho

Royce Hanson
Maggie Creek Ranch, Nevada

Tough and tender

Trayer Ranch, Kansas

He's so
cute.

Bill Boyd
San Emigdio Ranch, California

San Emigdio Ranch, California

"Now get in the trailer."

previous page
Lorna and John Steiner
Triangle Ranch, Idaho

Jason Raymond
Hirschy Ranch, Montana

Mike Seal and Harry the Cow Dog
Hoggan Ranch, Hamer, Idaho

Brett Reeder and Bob Marriott
Copper Basin, Idaho

The calf rescue

Kevin Donahue
Mackay, Idaho

"It's
my
stick!"

Yokohl Ranch, California

42

Claudia Gonzales, Vogt Ranch, California

Claudia Gonzales, Vogt Ranch, California

Vogt Ranch, Elk Creek, California

Only by the grace of
God go thee

LX Ranch, Texas

"I know I ain't pretty."

"Now
get
through
the darn
gate."

San Emigdio Ranch, California

"Thanks for the ride."

Chuch Hall and Johnny

Hall Ranch, Idaho

The old stare down

"We'll get 'em clean."

Colby Stoecklein, Lacy Zollinger, Lincoln Zollinger
Bar Horseshoe Ranch, Mackay, Idaho

Butch Arnold
Crockett, Texas

56

Crockett, Texas

"Let me out!"

Goin' to the beach

"OK, we worked at the branding, don't we get fed too?"

Regatti Ranch, California

"I know I'm no cow dog,
but I'm the boss
around this barn."

Vermedahl Ranch, Montana

"There I was minding my own business and then guess who jumped me and made me climb this dang fence?"

Mesa Pate and Reata
Pate Ranch, Montana

Mesa, Rial, and Tammy Pate with Reata
Pate Ranch, Montana

65

Art Robinson
Snowline Grazing Association, Montana

"If you didn't weigh so much
you could walk on
the snow too."

66

Lyle and Jonny Jordan
CA Ranch, Montana

Leonard Montez
San Emigdio Ranch, California

Time to practice

on the old dog.

John Vermedahl
Vermedahl Ranch, Montana

"What
would
he do
without
me?"

Shannon Meyers
Yokohl Ranch, California

Peggy Coolman
Venture Farms, Texas

"What he doesn't know won't hurt him."

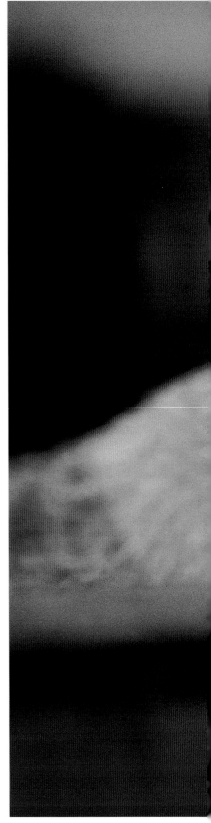

YO Ranch, Texas

Clockwise from top left: YP Ranch, Nevada; Smith Ranch, Idaho; Broken River Ranch, Idaho; Jayo Ranch, Idaho

Clockwise from top left: Twin Bridges, Montana; Zollinger Ranch, Idaho; Yokohl Ranch, California; Zollinger Ranch, Idaho

Old blue eyes

Trayer Ranch, Kansas

Trayer Ranch, Kansas

Getting a drink

Fred Reyes
Reyes Ranch, California

Fred Reyes
Reyes Ranch, California

"I should go over there and show that cowboy and silly horse how it's done."

San Emigdio Ranch, California

"Yeehaw! Now we're cowboyin'."

YO Ranch, Texas

Jim Murff
YO Ranch, Texas

Brett Zollinger
Zollinger Ranch, Idaho

"I wish I had me some of them warm boots!"

Christmas
Bar Horseshoe Ranch, Mackay, Idaho

"Why do I have to stay in the truck?"

Cornwell Ranch, Montana

Lynn Cornwell
Cornwell Ranch, Montana

San Emigdio Ranch, California

Rounding them up

"I hope I don't get caught."

Estrella Ranch, California

April Gordon and her Corgi
California

JA Ranch, Texas

"My puppy."

Brown Ranch, Texas

A little dusty

Roger Peters
Dragging Y Ranch, Montana

Steve Schroder
Dragging Y Ranch, Montana

King Ranch Cow Dogs

At the King Ranch, we use Border Collies to help our replacement heifers overcome their fear of men and unfamiliar surroundings such as corrals or working pens. Our cattle are range animals and see men only frequently—most often from a comfortable distance. Otherwise, the cattle come into contact with men in the working pens, where they are branded, vaccinated, or subjected to other uncomfortable procedures. Naturally, they become wary of close contact with men.

For reasons I do not know, the eight Border Collies we use have a calming effect on the cattle. Whereas a man on foot or on horseback will oftentimes cause the cattle to split into singles or small groups and try to get away, the dogs cause the cattle to bunch and herd together. When in a herd, the cattle become more calm and docile.

For this reason, at weaning, our replacement heifers are moved to a set of pastures where they are looked after by a caretaker who, with the dogs, trains the cattle to bunch, move forward, go through open gates, and follow the dog handler as he leads the cattle where he wants them to go.

The dogs work by subtly moving to the area from which the handler wants the cattle to move. The cattle will then move slowly away from the dogs. Occasionally, the dogs will nip the heels of a slow mover or the nose of an aggressive heifer that wants to fight, but they do not bark, growl, or howl. They simply move to an area and the heifers move away. The dogs then work back and forth, prompting the heifers to move in the direction of the caretaker, who is walking ahead of the herd toward the desired destination.

The dogs work from voice commands, hand signals, whistles, or a combination of these. It is rare for the dogs to excite the cattle or in any way attract attention to themselves. Late in the training period, the caretaker will travel on horseback while the dogs move the cattle, teaching them to follow a man on a horse.

—John Toelkes

Encarnacion "Chonito" Silva III
King Ranch, Texas

Bower Ranch, East Texas

102

Bower Ranch, East Texas

"Chasing wild cattle in the thick woods of East Texas makes you tough."

YO Ranch, Texas

"Wait for me."

"I said get back in the truck!"

Jessy Morgan, Chantelle Shields
Broken River Ranch, Idaho

"Hey, don't
squish me."

Ray Seal and Old Blue
Stanley, Idaho

Ray Seal and Old Blue
Stanley, Idaho

Taking a break

Frosty California morning

Yokohl Ranch, California

They come running right
little pat on the head

Yokohl Ranch, California

back and just wait for a

or a simple "good job."

Cornwell Ranch, Montana

Frank Willman with Reggie
Red Bluff, California

At the Red Bluff Bull, Gelding,
and Cow Dog Sale, dogs can
sell for as much as $8000.

Reggie and Taz
Red Bluff, California

Waiting for orders

Chet Vogt Ranch, California

Tejon Ranch, California

"I think this big
tongue is to
keep me cool."

Hollister Ranch, California

Lincoln Zollinger and Shade Rosenkrance
Mackay, Idaho

"Do these things bite?"

"Water? You don't have to be a Labrador."

Hall Ranch, Idaho

123

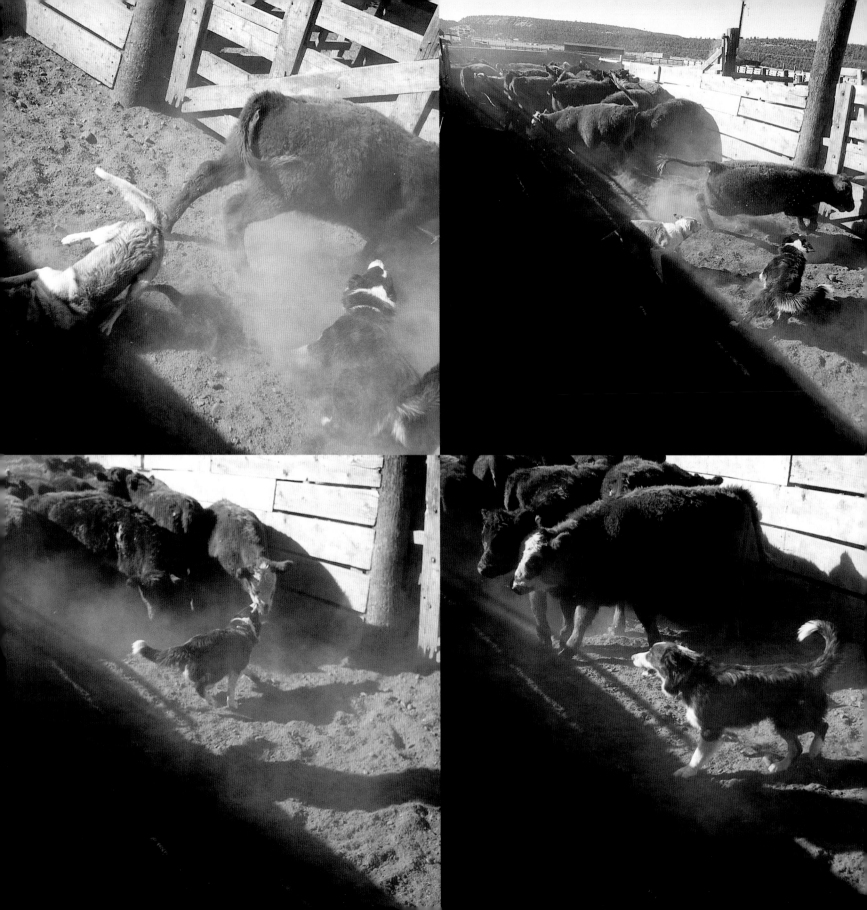

Working the chutes at the Flournoy Ranch

Jess Valley Ranch, California

125

Nipping at the heels

Russ Ranch, California

Lane Russ and his helpers
Russ Ranch, California

Thomas Saunders and Rick Wilson with Tom's dog, Peaches, loading up for work

Weatherford, Texas

Evening workout

Hollister Ranch
Santa Barbara, California

San Emigdio Ranch, California

Ready to go

San Emigdio Ranch, California

"The dentist told me not to chew on rocks."

Perry Quarter Horses
Ocala, Florida

"Now how about that biscuit?"

Perry Quarter Horses
Ocala, Florida

Dog-tired

Colby Stoecklein
Bar Horseshoe Ranch, Mackay, Idaho

"Can I keep all of these?"

Bibliography

American Border Collie Association
82 Rogers Road
Perkinston, MS 39573

The American Kennel Club
51 Madison Avenue
New York, NY 10016

The North American Sheep Dog Society
RR3
McLeansboro, IL 62859

The International Sheep Dog Society
Chesam House
47 Bromham Rd
Bedford, England MK40 2AA

The Australian National Kennel Council
Royal Show Grounds
Ascot Vale, Victoria, Australia

The United States Border Collie Club
12813 Maple St
Silver Spring, MD 20904

The Unites States Border Collie Handlers Association
Rt 1 Box 17A
Crawford, TX 76638
www.usbcha.com

American Kennel Club
260 Madison Ave.
New York, NY 10016

The United States Australian Shepherd Association
3510 Edmundson Rd
St. Louis, MO 63114

Australian Shepherd Club of America
PO Box 3790
Bryan, TX 77805

Australian National Kennel Council

Australian Cattle Dog Club of America

American Catahoula Association
PO Box 248
Abita Springs LA 70420

National Stockdog Registry
Butler, IN

The Working Kelpie Councile of Australia, Inc.
P. O. Box 306
Castle Hill
New South Wales, 1765 Australia

Thanks to the Dogs

As always, I thank the cowboys and their families for helping me in this endeavor. In addition, I want to give special thanks to all the dogs for their hard work. Their dedication to their families and to their jobs, along with their sense of wonder, diverse personalities, and tenacity, are what made this project possible.

Thanks,

David R. Stoecklein

I would like to dedicate this book to my brother Buzzie, who like a loyal dog has always been there for me.

Love, Dave